I Turned to See His Voice

Shirley Arnold

D1490596

I Turned to See His Voice
by Shirley Arnold

Printed in the United States of America
ISBN 1-931232-06-7

Xulon Press
344 Maple Ave. West, #302
Vienna, VA 22180
703-691-7595
XulonPress.com

Dedications & Acknowledgments

To all those who have been a part of bringing this part of revelation of hunger and divine desperation to book form.

To Jennifer for her tireless efforts to make the right connections and keep me on task.

To our ministry staff that handled the day-to-day issues to allow me time to write.

To the diligent seekers who have affected my life, Dorothy Clay, Jennifer Wilkes, Ron McIntosh, Varle & Buck Rollins, Joy Strang, Terry Thompson and Iverna Tompkins.

Special thanks to Dr. Larry Keefauver who encouraged me to do this book.

Last but certainly not least, to Steve, Stephanie, Michael, Melody & Michaela, who have always chosen the higher calling.

Table of Contents

Introduction

The destiny of the church is two-fold. First, we are predestined to be conformed to His image. Secondly, we are predestined to display His glory. Anything less is empty and unsatisfying to the diligent seeker. In the "purpose-driven" atmosphere of the church, there seems to be much activity and little fulfillment. The purpose of this book is to help bring definition to the desperate cry of the believer for the "real thing".

Our predestination for His likeness and His glory compels us to address every hindrance that keeps us from the revelation we crave – God Himself! It can be summed up in this truth. We are destined for change. But, true change can only occur when we behold the Lord. The hope of this book is to help the church recover her ability to see by removing the veils that cover her eyes.

"…when one turns to the Lord, the veil is taken away. Now the Lord is the Spirit; and where the Spirit of the Lord is, there is liberty. But we all, with unveiled face, beholding as in a mirror the glory of the Lord are being changed into the same image from glory to glory…" (II Cor. 3:16-18)

Chapter 1

Have You Seen the Voice?

I was in the Spirit on the Lord's Day, and I heard behind me a loud voice, as of a trumpet, saying, "I am the Alpha and the Omega, the First and the Last," and, "What you see, write in a book and send it to the seven churches which are in Asia: to Ephesus, to Smyrna, to Pergamos, to Thyatira, to Sardis, to Philadelphia, and to Laodicea." Then I turned to see the voice that spoke with me. And having turned I saw seven golden lampstands, and in the midst of the seven lampstands One like the Son of Man, clothed with a garment down to the feet and girded about the chest with a golden band. His head and hair were white like wool, as white as snow, and His eyes like a flame of fire; His feet were like fine brass, as if refined in a furnace, and His voice as the sound of many waters; He had in His right hand seven stars, out of His mouth went a sharp two-edged sword, and His countenance was like the sun shining in its strength. And when I saw Him, I fell at His feet as dead. (emphasis added. Revelation 1:10-17a)

I was surprised at the strength in my three-year-old daughter's soft, diminutive hands. My daughter had finally taken the situation into her own hands. Melody was sitting in my lap at a family gathering. I was carrying on several conversations at once. Amid the sounds of nieces and nephews playing and lunch preparations. Melody was trying to tell me something.

I heard a word here and there and gave an occasional pat on her leg to let her know I was hearing her. Somehow my sporadic acknowledgment did not satisfy her. With all her might Melody put one hand on each side of my face. One surprising jerk of my head brought me face to face with my daughter. She said, "Mommy, I want to see your mouth!" She was really asking for my full attention. She wanted to be certain I heard her words and responded. Never one to share me with others, she made a demand no other person in the room could make. And, she made her point. Melody would never be satisfied with occasional or casual contact. Nor can we be satisfied with just a casual relationship with God. Let me share with you another example of how we see His voice.

A similar experience happened to a friend of mine that helped him understand his relationship with God. He told me about his childhood memory. When he came home from school, he would spread his books on the coffee table, turn on the television and begin to do his homework. His mother would be busy in the kitchen when he arrived. From both sides of the kitchen door, they called out to one another greetings and the news of the day. Sometimes, he could hear his mother's voice, but could not understand her words.

After becoming a Christian he was often frustrated in his search to communicate with his Heavenly Father. One day the

Holy Spirit reminded him of the way he had communicated with his mother. He suddenly realized he had been talking with God as though He were in another room, out of sight. His cry out to the Lord, "I don't want to only know you are there. I don't want to only hear your voice occasionally from another room. I want to see, hear and know you face to face."

His desperate cry echoes the heart's cry of any believer who is unsatisfied with a casual pursuit of God. "But without faith it is impossible to please Him, for he who comes to God must believe that He is, and that He is a rewarder of those who diligently seek Him." The Greek word for diligently seek (*ekzeteo*) means to orient your will and entire life toward **aggressively pursuing** something or someone. It implies that you will search until you find, knock until a door is opened and ask until the answer comes.

For every believer, the object of his or her seeking is not an answer, a reward or an open door. Rather, believers seek whom not what. Whom do you diligently seek—Jesus! The intensity of the search may be compared with the focused, undeterred march of an army into battle. When we understand that we march in the end-time army of the King of kings, then we will become more than casual inquirers or distracted followers of every sign and wonder that surfaces whenever a new sensation comes to town. Rather, the soldiers standing shoulder to shoulder marching with the King in His kingdom will be motivated by an insatiable hunger both to seek and to see His face, exhibit His glory and be governed by His holiness.

John, a disciple of Jesus, was militantly committed to His Lord. When he became identified with Jesus, John was treated just like Jesus. Isn't that our hope? John was known as having been with Jesus (Acts 4:13). The religious zealots of the day were threatened by John's devotion to a man whom the religious leaders thought was dead and buried. Afraid that John's fiery devotion to Jesus would influence others to join in his belief, John's antagonists took him to court, found him guilty and sentenced him to exile on an island named Patmos. Deprived of everything and everyone he knew in the natural, the loyalty of his heart compelled him to continue to pursue the supernatural presence of the Lover of his soul—Christ the Lord.

Seeing His Voice

Revelation 1 tells the story of John's encounter, through a vision of Jesus Christ. First, he heard a voice that he describes sounded like a trumpet. Out of the sound of the trumpet, he heard a voice telling him to write a message to the churches. However, in verse 12 John makes an interesting statement. He says, "I turned to see the voice." We might ask…

- Wasn't the voice enough?
- Wasn't the sound of a trumpet enough?
- Why did John turn?

Perhaps John's response was born out of the same desperate hunger you and I share for "more." John turned to see the voice. He wanted to see the One who was speaking to him. No longer satisfied with hearing alone, John wanted to exercise all his spiritual senses—including spiritual sight.

Reading through the book of Revelation, one truth becomes strikingly clear. John not only wrote about things he heard; he also wrote about what he saw and experienced. The revelation of Jesus Christ could never be expressed in one dimension.

Diligently seeking Christ can never be one-dimensional. Once we have heard about Him, we want to hear Him. Once we have learned about Him, we want earnestly to know Him. And once we have pictured the visions that others have of Him, we must see Him for ourselves. John had earlier written of this tangible, multi-dimensional encounter with Christ in his first letter.

> *That which was from the beginning, which we have heard, which we have seen with our eyes, which we have looked upon, and our hands have handled, concerning the Word of life—the life was manifested, and we have seen, and bear witness, and declare to you that eternal life which was with the Father and was manifested to us—that which we have seen and heard we declare to you, that you also may have fellowship with us; and truly our fellowship is with the Father and with His Son Jesus Christ. (1 John 1:1-3)*

Notice that John wrote of hearing, seeing, gazing intently upon and touching the Word of God—Jesus Christ. All of a person's being should encounter the Word of life. In fact, if a believer only experiences in one dimension, that encounter will be lacking, superficial and empty. Let me explain with an analogy.

Our nation's obsession with health and weight loss comes as a result of our poor eating habits. Namely, our addiction to junk food. It tastes so good in our mouth, but provides no real nutrition to our body. It is empty food. "Junk" food has the look, feel and taste that makes us want more. Why? Scientists take real food and manipulate them with salt, sugar, caffeine and grease. Cultures around the world are being contaminated with this instant gratification. It seems the worse it is, the more we want it. Millions have been spent developing the best french fry.

Some adults don't really like fast food. Never fear. Children are lured into restaurants with games, toys, playgrounds and anything else that will get the parent addicted. It can make our stomachs feel full and add inches to our waistlines, but never feed the hunger for the nutrients our bodies crave.

Many Christians experience empty lives because we have been on a fast food diet of empty religion and empty pursuit. Our spirits are crying out for what will truly feed the hunger of our desperation to experience more than a voice. We must see the Voice that speaks to us.

In the days of Samuel, the Bible declares the word of the LORD was rare. "Then the boy Samuel ministered to the LORD before Eli. And the word of the LORD was rare in those days; there was no widespread revelation (1 Samuel 3:1). Thank God that is no longer true. We live in a day when the word of the LORD is readily available. However, we are tempted to seek His voice with no regard for personal responsibility. What should be our personal responsibility? With the restoration of the office of the prophet and the release of the prophetic giftings, we can switch channels from voice to voice as easily as seeking channels on a radio. We are "ever learning and never able to come to the knowledge of the truth" (2 Timothy 3:7).

We Need a Revelation of His Voice

When John turned to look at the Voice, he saw Jesus standing in the middle of the lampstands which represented the churches. The Voice was revealed in the midst of the church. That places the responsibility of the seeing of His voice right in the middle of the Body of Christ, not in the midst of casual gatherings of disinterested seekers, who may fail to see His voice because of their own distractions or agendas. Our hearts desire should be to gather with other believers who, like ourselves, passionately seek after Jesus.)

What is it that we diligently seek? *To see His voice.* How is that manifested? "And the Word became flesh and dwelt among us, and we beheld His glory, the glory as of the only begotten of the

Father, full of grace and truth" (John 1:14). Where will that happen? When two or more are gathered in a local body in His name. "For where two or three are gathered together in My name, I am there in the midst of them" (Matthew 18:20).

Therefore, the local church has the responsibility to create a prophetic atmosphere which brings a revelation of Jesus and His Voice. In the local church, safety and accountability exist through the governmental order God has ordained. Because many local fellowships have not given opportunity to the development of prophetic ministry, individual believers have been searching for a voice anywhere they can find a voice. Such random searching, instead of diligent seeking, reminds me of the children of Israel who wanted to hear from God, but weren't willing to go through the process of finding God.

> Now all the people witnessed the thunderings, the lightning flashes, the sound of the trumpet, and the mountain smoking; and when the people saw it, they trembled and stood afar off. Then they said to Moses, "You speak with us, and we will hear; but let not God speak with us, lest we die." And Moses said to the people, "Do not fear; for God has come to test you, and that His fear may be before you, so that you may not sin." So the people stood afar off, but Moses drew near the thick darkness where God was. (Exodus 20:18-21)

The Israelites were contented with sending Moses to the mountain to bring back a message from God. Their desire for "fast-food" empty experiences of God did not give them the spiritual nutrients they needed to develop and grow strong. They were willing to have a second-hand knowledge of God instead of seeing, hearing and encountering Him up close and personal. As a result of their failure to diligently seek him, they quickly searched for a god-substitute when Moses was delayed on the mountain.

The golden calf idol, satisfied Israel because they had not been willing to wait for God. Moses' encounter with the Living God was not enough to sustain them. They believed in the God of Moses. They saw the results of God's presence. But, believing in God and living in a personal revelation of God are two different things. The same is true for us. No one else's revelation of God can sustain us.

How Boldly are You Seeking to See His Voice?

John's act of turning to see the Voice demonstrated amazing courage. Jesus did not tell him to turn around. Jesus simply instructed him to write what he saw. John could have waited for a vision, but His first priority was to see the author of the vision. He made a demand on the voice. Just like my little Melody wanted to see my mouth, John wanted to see Jesus' mouth.

Sometimes, I think we are too timid in our approach to God.

Scripture counsels just the opposite, "Let us therefore come boldly to the throne of grace, that we may obtain mercy and find grace to help in time of need" (Heb. 4:16). So, John reacted in boldness and determination. Too often, we confuse our timidity with reverence.

Many have the view that we must tiptoe around the LORD in the eastern fashion of keeping bent-over postures and never looking directly upon the King. This kind of thinking is absolutely wrong in light of God's open invitation. It is not only our right to see His voice; it's a command.

Other examples in addition to John may be found in Scripture of those boldly seeking God. One night a man named Jacob had an encounter with an angel of the Lord. He began to wrestle with that angel. In fact, it became an all-night wrestling match. As the sun was rising, the angel made an effort to leave. Jacob boldly grabbed hold of the angel and declared his intention. He told the angel he would not let him go until he had received a blessing.

> And He [*the angel of the Lord*] said, "*Let Me go, for the day breaks.*" *But he* [*Jacob*] *said, "I will not let You go unless You bless me!" So He said to him, "What is your name?" And he said, "Jacob." And He said, "Your name shall no longer be called Jacob, but Israel; for you have struggled with God and with men, and have prevailed." (Gen. 32:26-28)*

Apparently, Jacob wanted his all night challenge to result in something valuable. I am not sure many of us would have the boldness to forbid an angel to leave! There's something about struggling through the dark times of life that strips away our visitation. By the time we have wrestled with our challenges and faced our fears, we want something to show for it!

Moses was known as a friend of God. The very nature of true friendship involves interaction and intimacy. Moses knew Him as a face-to-face God. But, his boldness before God would scare most of us. In Exodus 33, Moses argued with the LORD concerning who would assist him in leading the children of Israel to the Promised Land. In no uncertain terms, Moses made it clear he would not take one more step unless God went with him. He refused angelic help because he considered angels to be a substitute for the presence of God. When Jehovah relented and made the promise that His presence would go with him, Moses was encouraged to an even bolder step. Having received God's favor, Moses pressed in for more. "Show me your glory . . ."

> So the LORD said to Moses, "I will also do this thing that you have
> spoken; for you have found grace in My sight, and I know you by
> name." And he said, "Please, show me Your glory." Then He said,
> "I will make all My goodness pass before you, and I will proclaim
> the name of the LORD before you. I will be gracious to whom I will
> be gracious, and I will have compassion on whom I will have

compassion." But He said, "You cannot see My face; for no man shall see Me, and live." And the Lord *said, "Here is a place by Me, and you shall stand on the rock. "So it shall be, while My glory passes by, that I will put you in the cleft of the rock, and will cover you with My hand while I pass by. "Then I will take away My hand, and you shall see My back; but My face shall not be seen."* (Exodus 33:17-23)

Moses was not content with just climbing a mountain and meeting initially with God to receive the Torah. He wanted more! Moses boldly pressed in and diligently sought God with audacity and boldness. How many times do we miss a fuller revelation because we are content with the initial revelation? If Moses had settled for the mountain-top revelation of God, he would have missed seeing God in His glory.

Many of us are uncomfortable with the concept that we should place a demand on our wonderful Heavenly Father. However, Scripture often records the actions of desperate people pushed to boldness.

- Joshua lingered in the presence of God.
- Ruth sought God's purpose for her destiny by risking her reputation in approaching Boaz.
- David pressed into the heart of God.
- Isaiah entered into the holiness of God.

- Esther risked her life on behalf of God's plan for His people.
- Peter so hungered to be with Jesus he boldly walked on water.
- Stephen peered into heaven itself as he courageously died for his King.

All were desperately, diligently and boldly seeking God. So what made John turn to see the voice? What made Jacob hold on for his blessing? What made Moses refuse the substitution that God offered? Why didn't the saints of old simply settle for the little of god they had instead of risking all for more?

The motivation that separated the diligent seeker from the casual inquirer could be called hunger or curiosity. Indeed, my own hunger has gone beyond simple curiosity. Has yours? Like John, Jacob, Moses, and all the saints of old, I can no longer be satisfied with a one-dimensional view of God. I am desperately seeking to see His voice.

Perhaps you have that same desperation, or maybe you feel that . . .

- where you've come to in seeking God isn't far enough.
- what you hear can't suffice and you need to see the One who is talking to you.

- clichés and religious sound bites do not satisfy your desperate yearning to know Him.
- experiencing God second hand through the testimonies of others doesn't fill your need to experience Him first-hand.
- the glory you've seen on others only makes you hunger more for His transforming power to change you from glory to glory.

So what are you waiting for? With John, turn now to see His voice.

Chapter 2

Desperate People Do Desperate Things

T he scene was surreal. My family huddled together in our front yard. Amidst the drizzle of freezing rain, we could see the pre-dawn light appearing. The only warmth we felt came as the flames of our burning home intensified. The frenzied moments of our family's escape had given way to a calm numbness. It felt as though we were on the outside looking in on a screen of our lives. The desperation of those first moments had already changed our lives forever.

The miracle had not escaped our notice. Our whole family was sound asleep when I bolted upright in the bed around 5:00 a.m. I smelled smoke. Statistically, people who are sleeping never smell smoke. They simply inhale the poisonous gas until it is too late.

When my husband, Steve, and I discovered smoke in our house, we did not care about our furniture, our clothes or our personal belongings. The only thought we had was to get to our two babies who were sleeping in another bedroom down the hall. My grandmother's cherished antique hutch did not receive one single thought as I made my way down the smoke-filled corridor to my daughters. After grabbing hold of the girls and making our way outside, we waited for the fire trucks to come.

We stood in the front yard and watched the flames grow more intense by the moment. We were aware that the raging fire was destroying our household belongings. We could hear the roof falling in as the fire methodically destroyed everything in its path.

However, even as we witnessed this devastating event, we experienced no feeling of loss. Our babies were in our arms, our family was safe, and we were content. The desperation of this crisis had quickly changed the definition of our priorities.

Most of us can look back upon certain moments in which our lives were changed because of a "paradigm interruption." What's a paradigm? Paradigms are the boxes that hold our perceptions. For example, two people see the same car wreck between an elderly person and a teenager. In reality, both drivers only slowed down at a four-way stop and proceeded almost simultaneously to drive through the intersection without noticing the other vehicle. Both witnesses have seen the exact same accident standing at the same corner. How they process what they see is shaped by their own personal paradigms. One witness holds fast to the paradigm that all teenagers are reckless drivers. The other witness has a paradigm that strongly holds to the notion that elderly people cannot respond quickly to unexpected driving situations. So, the first witness' paradigm shapes his perception that the teen driver was at fault while the second witness believes just as strongly that the elderly person caused the accident. For both witnesses, their perceptions were deposited into their own paradigm box that produced different conclusions.

So a paradigm is a mindset, a way of viewing reality which has been shaped by your own beliefs, experiences and knowledge. Our internal paradigms set our priorities, shape our perceptions and influence our responses to life. Our paradigm of a quiet, uninterrupted life that was physically connected to inherited memorabilia and preserved artifacts quickly went up in smoke as the flames burned a new reality into our minds. The paradigm that shaped what we had comfortably thought God was doing in our lives changed forever.

God's Ways Challenge Us to Change Our Ways

Our ways of thinking and the unintentional boundaries we set in our pursuit of God will never be enlarged without a confrontation. *We will continue in business as usual unless we are challenged to change.* Human nature does not grasp beyond the obvious to the unknown. Our natural lifestyle promotes this way of thinking at all costs. Our goals reflect our quest for more comfort and more luxury. Change threatens to dismantle our paradigm of comfort. Let me give you an example.

Have you ever tried to buy a new mattress? It is mind-boggling to look at the number of options available. The questions are never-ending. How many springs per square inch? How thick do you want the padding? What patterns do you want on the cover? Do the sides offer enough support to avoid sagging? What you find is that you can have the amount of comfort you can afford. Anything is possible if you have enough money.

Most of the mattresses are sufficient for sleeping. But, we may come to believe that some are more sufficient than others.

Several levels of comfort are available to us. So, ideally, we begin at the level we can afford and seek to prosper that we may afford a higher level of comfort. This obsession with comfort resists anything that may require denial. We feel it is our God-given, American right to grasp for the brass ring of a comfort-filled lifestyle instead of Spirit-filled lifestyle. *We need a continual challenge to keep us from settling into our comfort zone and slowing down our pursuit of God.*

When our daughters were five & seven years old, my husband and I took them on a November missions trip to Eastern Europe. The oppression of communism hung heavily in the atmosphere. Those were the days when Germany was still divided by the Berlin Wall into East and West Germany. The "Iron Curtain" country of Poland was under martial law and suffering. People stood in line as everything was rationed. They received only a couple of pounds of meat per month. Toiletries such as toilet paper and soap were rationed and almost non-existent. Just the rumor of a product becoming available in a certain location would cause lines to form all during the night, even on snowy, frigid nights. One pound of American coffee was worth the equivalent of $100 American dollars. The average income for a Polish family was between $20-$30 American dollars per month. We knew our Polish Christian friends had been saving their rations for meat for several months as they anticipated our arrival. They wanted to serve us good meals while we ministered among them.

Our hosts were a precious pastor, his wife and their two children. We lived in their home for two weeks. Their children and ours became good friends as they spent their days playing together in the small apartment we all shared. Our children were surprised at the lack of toys their new friends had. Our girls brought more toys in their backpack to keep them occupied during the long plane trip, than their new friends had in their home. When we returned home, Christmas preparations were upon us.

As part of our normal Christmas tradition, we asked the girls for their wish list. To our surprise, they had nothing on their lists. Apparently, those days in Poland had brought them to a paradigm shift. Their closet full of toys seemed sufficient after observing the plight of their new Polish friends. *Being confronted with someone else's lack had a tremendous impact on priorities.*

Any short or long-term missionary will tell you the same story. Our valuable things suddenly lose their value to us when we see the needs of others. Our priorities are challenged and our way of thinking is enlarged. We will not change unless our motivation overpowers our paradigm for comfort. Until we reach a true desperation, we will continue to operate in the same familiar pattern. *Desperation can be the defining element that promotes us from a "good" place in God to the place of His strategic destiny.*

From a Good Place to God's Place in Destiny

John the Revelator was in a "good" place in God. He was actively serving the Lord with a powerful witness. His witness was so powerful he drew the attention of the ruling authorities and became a threat to the status quo. For all practical purposes He was a "good" witness in a "good" ministry having "good" results. With no confrontation, he could have spent his life never knowing the difference between "good" and "best." His arrest and consequent exile could not have seemed to be the hand of God strategically placing Him in the center of his destiny.

The result of John's exile was that he had to leave everything familiar. Familiarity entombs us in sameness. When we are shaken from the false sense of security that we may find in people, place and position, we realize the futility of pursuing stability outside of His presence. *The only constant we can count on is change!*

No longer buried in the familiar and nothing to hold on to, John became a desperate man. He was a man with new priorities. *His ministry became less important than his need to know the God of his ministry.*

If you are truly a militant seeker, get ready for God to challenge the familiar in your life. The familiar is like a comfortable, old shoe. It has conformed to our foot shape and it is comfortably broken in to our way of walking. But if God calls you to run instead of walk or to walk in a different way, the old shoe simply won't fit the change He has for you. If you love comfort and familiarity, your fear of confrontation and change could inhibit your search for the greater revelation.

Remember the Israelites wandering through the wilderness after God had freed them from slavery in Egypt? Israel had grown comfortable in slavery. The Israelites had certain foods they ate and familiar ways to address problems in life. They had grown used to their bondages and did not miss the liberties they had never known. The price of wilderness freedom was change and change to their paradigm of comfort. They often cried out to return to Egypt preferring bondage to change. At times, we find ourselves like the ancient Israelites—desiring to return to our comfortable paradigms rather than facing the unknown and often surprising challenges of change through which God frees us and equips us for His purposes.

God's Change Compels Us to Desperately Seek New Priorities

The familiar shapes its own paradigms and carries its own set of priorities. When God begins to compel us into new places, old priorities lose their importance. We begin to operate in a new priority system.

Have you ever noticed how our prayer lives change in the midst of crisis? Suddenly, our unmotivated confessions of faith become urgent in their tone. In fact, our prayer times may become less talking and more listening. Why? Because we have become desperate for a word from God. Our priority has changed from telling Him about the problem to hearing what He has to say about the answer.

Moses found himself in a paradigm confrontation. He had become a desperate man. He was a Hebrew raised as Egyptian royalty and one day he witnessed an Egyptian taskmaster beating a Hebrew slave. Enraged, Moses murdered the Egyptian. After learning that his crime had been witnessed by other Hebrew slaves, Moses desperately fled into the wilderness. His comfortable way of life had been radically changed. His paradigm for understanding reality as royalty shifted to a nomadic shepherd's way of life. Talk about change! Moses had to adjust over night to a completely different lifestyle. He had been plunged into a desperate situation that would ultimately lead him to an encounter with his God.

While tending his flock of sheep one day, he saw a bush that was burning but not consumed. Moses turned to see a voice speaking out of a burning bush. He became a man with his feelings of inadequacy. When God called to him out of the burning bush, his only hesitations had to do with identity. He felt inadequate to do what he was called to do. His fear of rejection by Pharaoh and by his people caused him to question God's choosing him as a mouthpiece to the Hebrews.

So, Moses asked for help in delivering the children of Israel. In spite of his wrath with Moses, God sanctioned Aaron, Moses' brother, to speak for him. Even before Moses doubted himself, he said to God, "...behold, when I come unto the children of Israel, and shall say unto them, the God of our Fathers has said unto you; and they shall say to me, What is His name? What shall I say unto them? And God said unto Moses, I AM THAT I AM" (Exodus 3:14).

God's revelation should have settled all the questions. But, Moses had a need for acceptance and a fear of failure. Even though he was called and chosen, he still had some lessons to learn. After the children of Israel were finally released from Egypt, the adventure began in earnest. No matter what Moses did, it wasn't enough to please them. They complained about the food, the water and the leadership.

The burden of hearing the people's constant murmuring and experiencing their lack of obedience to God's commands brought Moses to a crisis in Exodus 33. The time had come to move the nation again. But, Moses felt alone and abandoned. He had put his trust in Aaron and Miriam. They had proven to be unworthy of his trust. This nation he had been called to deliver rejected him and his leadership.

Moses was no longer asking for another man to represent him and speak for him. It no longer mattered to him whether he had acceptance or not. Somewhere on that journey his priorities had changed. He was now looking for God's approval and only His.

What a blessed relief it is when man's opinions no longer chart our course. However, it is often a painful journey that brings us to the end of our need for approval from men and our desire that craves to know Him and Him alone.

Our Desperation Drives Us to Seek Only God's Approval

It's hard to believe that our disappointment in others is actually the seedbed of discovery. I walked through a season several years ago when it seemed that every significant relationship in my life was hurting me. Even in the leadership arena, I saw things in minister's lives that shocked and appalled me. People I respected and trusted were proving to be frail humanity. I said to the Lord, "I'm so disillusioned." His response to me was surprising. He said, "Good. Now I've got you where I want you."

To be disillusioned means to come to the end of an illusion. It was an illusion to think that I would never suffer rejection at the hands of those I loved. It is an illusion to think ministers are perfect and never make mistakes. I realized I had placed an inordinate demand upon people to give me what only my Father could give. A process began to bring about a change in my priorities. Instead of seeking after the approval of man, my first priority became to seek God's approval.

One of the ways God will deal with our need for approval is to put us in a place where it is impossible to receive what we think we need. As a minister, I had to get this thing settled early.

In any given meeting, there will be a percentage of the congregation who do not particularly identify or agree with me. There will be a percentage that could take or leave my ministry. And there will be a percentage (hopefully, the majority) who will be touched and changed by the ministry flow in my life.

When I first started out traveling, I tried hard to make everyone like me. My messages were full of attempts to include everyone. I tried to make sure I would say nothing offensive. I was in complete bondage to my need for acceptance. Even though I continued to cater to the disgruntled, there was always someone who would approach me after service with a dissenting question or a comment.

One inevitable question that would always seem to arise concerned women in the pulpit. I tried to answer the question with a solid scriptural understanding. However, one question would lead to another until I found myself engaged in useless debate. It finally occurred to me that there will always be people who don't believe in women ministers, and I can't make them accept me.

This rang all too true while my husband and I were in Romania many years ago. I had the opportunity to minister in many churches where no woman had ever ministered before. I wasn't allowed to stand on the platform and had to wear a scarf on my head, but I was thrilled for the opportunity. In one particular service, a man was brought for healing who could not walk or talk because of a brain operation. One side of his head was sunken in and his eyes were glassy and fixed. While praying for him, we experienced the powerful work of the Holy Spirit. This man's head began to fill out and he began to speak and was soon able to walk. You can imagine the sense of awe and joy that filled that sanctuary.

After this glorious occurrence, we were being escorted through the crowd to our car. As we approached the door of the church, three men were waiting to talk to me. These men were elders of the church and they had an issue with me. They felt it was out of order for a woman to be praying for a man. I shook my head in disbelief and simply walked to the car and we drove away. After riding in silence for several minutes, I began to weep. I had thought that someday the anointing would be strong enough and the miracles would be great enough that there would never be another encounter with someone who did not receive me as a minister. So, I had to make a decision. I could no longer minister under the yoke of people's opinions. I minister, preach, sing and pray for the approval of an audience of one. *Only one opinion can matter to me—My Father's!!*

I would not be truthful if I said I did not appreciate being blessed by the congregation's acceptance. I'm always gratified when someone acknowledges his or her life is changed by the word of the LORD through the ministry. Thank God for the encouragement of the saints. But my heart is longing for the nod of my

Father's head in approval and the touch of His hand on my back.

Your Disappointment Can Lead You to Desperation for God

Have you been disappointed in a relationship? Has church leadership hurt you? Perhaps God is allowing you the perfect motivation to run hard after Him. This could be your moment of freedom from the exhausting merry-go-round of man's approval. Disappointment can serve to purify your motivation. It can lead you to a wonderful place of rest. You can find acceptance in the secret place of God — under the shadow of His approval.

Is it wrong to trust people? Absolutely not! But it is wrong to *need* their approval even more than Father God's. We are called to be members one to another. We can never be isolated from the body of Christ if we want to grow and help to establish God's Kingdom. The difference is priorities. Whose smile do you want to win?

Desperation Demand: DO WHATEVER IT TAKES!

Desperate people do whatever it takes. The woman with the issue of blood is a classic example (Mark 5). As the crowds pressed around Jesus, she saw that it was virtually impossible to get to Him. So, she dropped to the ground and began to weave herself through the crowd. Dust and dirt were everywhere. People were stepping on her and tearing her clothes as she made her way. She caught a glimpse of the fringe of His prayer shawl, his *talit*.

No matter how much dirt she had to eat or how many dirty feet stepped on her, she would not be denied. For twelve years she had gone to every doctor available and had spent all her money. She knew it was her last and only chance as she grabbed hold of the hem of His garment. Jesus knew desperation had touched Him.

In Matthew 15, a Canaanite woman approached Jesus to heal her daughter. Jesus gently rebuffed her with the news that He had been sent to the lost sheep of the house of Israel. How easily pride could have stolen her miracle. This woman swallowed her pride and pressed into Jesus immediately. She may have been the wrong nationality, but she knew she had the attention of the only person who could heal her daughter. Her refusal to leave Him alone gained her heart's desire. Jesus said, "Oh woman, great is your faith! Let it be to you, as you desire. And her daughter was healed from that very hour" (Matthew 15:28). Her desperation led her to Jesus.

Are you desperate enough yet to be driven away from your comfortable paradigms and into the presence of God? When your desperation grows stronger than your fear of change, you will reach out to touch Jesus!

Interestingly, once you have experienced desperation, you are now ready to make a demand on God. Both the woman with the issue of blood and the Canaanite woman demanded something from Jesus—and He responded! When you become desperate enough, you will be motivated by a new found boldness in His presence. It's time to make a demand!

Chapter 3

Make Your Demand

Y ou could call Jeremiah desperate! Called into ministry with a glorious word from God, Jeremiah's purpose was settled even before he was formed in his mothers' womb. He would be a prophet to the nations and would make a mighty impact on his own nation as well. Everything sounded so good in the beginning. But as time passed Jeremiah became aware that the call of God, glorious as it may be, was making certain difficult demands he had not expected.

On one occasion, he delivered a stinging rebuke to the priests of Topheth. They were so angry that they threw him in jail hoping to persuade him to change his prophetic word. When he was released the priests were looking for a new word, but Jeremiah could only say what God said which greatly displeased the religious authorities. While being persecuted for telling the truth, Jeremiah began to question his calling and the God who had called him. Desperate to understand what was happening to him, he cried out to God in Jeremiah 20:7-9:

"O Lord, Thou hast deceived me and I was deceived; Thou hast overcome me and prevailed. I have become a laughingstock all day long; everyone mocks me. For each time I speak, I cry aloud; I proclaim violence and destruction, Because for me the word of the LORD has resulted in reproach and derision all day long. But if I say, 'I will not remember Him or speak anymore in His name,' Then in my heart it becomes like a burning fire shut up in my bone; and I am weary of holding it in, and I cannot endure it." Jeremiah 20:7-9

Divine Entrapment

In other words, Jeremiah was saying, *I get in trouble if I tell the truth, but everything in me suffers if I don't tell the truth*. Some of us can identify with Jeremiah's dilemma. I call it *divine entrapment*. God never tells you the whole story in the beginning. He wisely knows that our frailty and fear of failure would cause us to miss out on His purpose for our lives if we knew the future. Caught up in the glimpse of His glory ruins you for the mediocre and the ordinary.

Even though Jeremiah was complaining, he knew he was divinely trapped. What could he go back to? Much like the disciples' response to Jesus when the offended crowds left Him. His statement concerning true communion included the instruction to eat His flesh and drink His blood (John 6:56). Of course, this statement was to be understood and applied spiritually. However, the crowds were unspiritual and undiscerning. Jesus turned to His friends and asked them if they were going to leave Him also. Their response declared the reality of their predicament, "Lord, to whom shall we go? You have words of eternal life. And we have believed and have come to know that You are the Holy One of God." (John 6: 68-69). There was no one else to follow and no where else to go.

Desperation Results in a Demand

Jeremiah's purpose was to call the nation to return to God. Their stubborn refusal to heed the word of the LORD was a source of continual frustration and persecution for the prophet. In Jeremiah 33, he was in prison for the second time. Desperately alone, the voice of God spoke to Him, "Call to Me, and I will answer you, and I will tell you great and mighty things, which you do not know" (v. 3). God's response to Jeremiah's desperation was an open invitation for him to make a demand on Him.

God's invitation to Jeremiah was something like this, "If you want to see something beyond this moment of distress, then call on Me! Don't sit in the mire of feeling sorry for yourself. Call on me! Make a demand on Me!"

Does that sound presumptuous to you? Presumption would demand that to which one is not entitled. Access to God's presence is the entitlement of every believer. You will notice that I did not say His presence is deserved. The presence of the LORD is a precious gift and privilege, never a deserved right. It is the hungry heart wooed by God Himself to explore and discover every facet of His nature.

God did not instruct Jeremiah to look for another prophet, nor even to seek a word from Him. He simply told him to call upon his God and all that he needed would be given to Him.

The answer God gave to Jeremiah was a prophetic promise that his life was not lived in vain. There would come a day when the places of desolation and destruction would be restored. The nation's rebellion and constant suffering would one day be turned into the voice of gladness when the day of restoration came. Our Father longs to reassure us and give us hope. *As we seek after the peace of God, we must be careful to make a demand on the One who is our peace.*

How Do We Demand of God?

Several years ago I was faced with a tremendous faith challenge. The doctor had just diagnosed me with an incurable, chronic disease. The prognosis was so discouraging it took my breath away. I was a woman raising two children with a wonderful husband and a thriving ministry. We were born again and part of a faith-filled church. Great men and women of God taught us dynamic principles of faith which we implemented everyday of our lives. Thank God for the faith message and those teachers who mightily trained us in the way of faith.

Somewhere along the way of our faith journey, we began to operate in a mistaken belief that we could get what we wanted by demanding God to answer according to our desire. We spouted the scriptures that God will give us the desires of our heart as proof we had a right to demand (cf. Psalm 37:4). Our faith was in faith itself. We knowingly constructed a faith-formula that we believed could never fail if we believed strongly enough.

You can already imagine the disastrous scenario produced from this kind of a belief system. With so much emphasis placed on the person and the method, it becomes easy to fix blame when the desired results are not forthcoming. When God does not perform the way we want, the natural conclusion is that our faith must have been weak or our method flawed. There are too many of these kinds of tragedies in the body of Christ. It has caused us to lose our ability to believe God, especially in the area of the miraculous.

So, with the doctor's diagnosis in hand, Steve and I began to put our faith to work. We followed all the formulas we knew. We put our trust in our faith. It had worked before. We had no doubt it would work again. However, as time passed, my symptoms began to worsen. Nothing we tried seemed to work. Completely bedridden and feeling like a failure, I began to question my methods. My demands for God to perform at my command were ringing more hollow and less true. There was an increasing dissatisfaction in my soul.

Up to this point, my faith would not allow me to take my guard down. There was a sense deep inside me that I was being called to a place of rest and trust. But, I was afraid any change of tactics would show a lack of faith. God's voice grew louder until it was undeniable that God wanted me to lay down all expectation - except in Him. This began a journey in an uncharted territory for us. Our trust was not based in our activity, but in His ability. My demands were no longer on the manifestation of healing, but on His presence.

Seeking Both God's Face and His Hand

As our hunger increased to see His voice, I heard someone say; "We should seek His face and not His hand." Does one exclude the other? The children of Israel only knew the acts of God while Moses knew His ways. Don't the ways of God include the acts of God?

Moses cried out to the LORD in Exodus 33 that he would not lead the people without the presence of the LORD going with them. This demand on the presence yielded a favorable response: "And He said, 'My presence shall go with you, and I will give you rest'" (v. 14). The word presence is *paniym* in the Hebrew. Its literal meaning is "faces." In other words, the presence of God meant that Moses would have all the faces of God going with him.

If Moses needed healing, then the face of the healer would be with Him. If he needed provision, the face of the provider would be evident. If he needed deliverance, comfort, etc, the God who is our all in all is sufficient. When I make a demand on the presence of God, all His faces are available to me. He is the answer and He has the answer.

What faces of God do you need? If you are to make a demand on His presence, do you desire Him or just the provision you need? In His presence, before His face, every need is met and every gift is given. Your demand has one object—His Presence, all of His faces. Are you willing to seek both His hand and His face?

I grew up in religious circles where it was considered more holy to "seek the giver instead of the gift." That kind of mindset seems to discount the gift. It gave some people a good excuse for their lack of participation in the gifts of the Holy Spirit. The Bible is clear that we should "seek earnestly the best gifts" (1 Cor. 14). The real issue is rooted in the heart's motivation. If I seek the gift or the manifestations of God without a heart's desire for His whole character, then I become a loud, clanging cymbal with no real substance at the very least. At its worst, I can become self-righteous in believing the gifts of God prove that I have somehow arrived.

On the other hand, if I seek the face of God with no regard to His hand, my pursuit could become very selfish and even prideful. Seeking the face of God will always move the hand of God. There should be no debate between the "face-seekers" or the "hand-seekers." As we make a demand on His presence, we are pursuing all that He is and all that He does.

When We Demand, God Meets Us

The whole concept that Father encourages us to make a demand on Him may make you a little uncomfortable. However, in situation after situation, the principle is clear. When Jesus met with the Samaritan woman at the well in John 4, He set her up to make a demand. His first words to her, "Give me a drink," set her up for a destiny encounter. She was surprised at His request. She did not believe she was qualified to fill His request for three very good reasons:

1. **She was a Samaritan.** Pious Jews had nothing to do with Samaritans. The Samaritan race existed because Jews intermarried with another race. A good Jew considered interaction with a Samaritan an abomination.

2. **She was a woman.** Women did not enjoy a particularly high level of esteem. One confession a Jewish man could be heard proclaiming in his morning prayers went something like this, "Thank God I was not born a woman, a Gentile or a dog."

3. **She was a woman of bad reputation.** Here was a woman who had been married five times and was now living with a man. She was familiar with stares, gossip and rejection. What could this friendly man mean by engaging her in conversation?

Jesus was breaking the rules of propriety. But, He was really doing more than that. He was placing a demand on a disqualified woman. She felt inadequate and unsure, certain He had made a mistake.

In John 4:10 we find the key to making a demand on God. Jesus said, " If you knew the gift of God, and who it is who says to you, 'Give Me a drink,' you would have asked Him, and He would have given you living water."

He was saying that if she only knew the One who was asking

her for a drink, she would have known this principle. *God will never ask you for something that He is not willing to supply to you.*

Our pursuit of Him is the direct result of His pursuit of us. When Father begins to make a demand on you, His purpose is to draw you to Himself as the One who will enable you.

Many years ago, the LORD gave us a vision for a leadership restoration and training facility. He told me to call it the Secret Place. He described it to me in much detail. It would house a school of ministry, missions network and a place to bring restoration to wounded and worn-out leaders. Seeing the vision was exhilarating. Bringing the vision to pass was exhausting! For seven years after receiving the word our family believed and prayed for it's fulfillment. As time went along, the vision became more of a dream than a reality. We believed God would perform His word "someday." On a beautiful July Sunday afternoon, "someday" turned into "today."

While glancing through a real estate magazine I picked up at a convenience store, I was captured by a picture of a house with this caption below. "Turn this albatross into a gold mine." With our curiosity piqued, we called the realtor. He met us at the property that afternoon. As our family toured the house, we were overwhelmed with six bedrooms, ten bathrooms, a media room, 2-lane bowling alley, swimming pool and indoor racquetball court.

With 14,000 square feet under roof, this massive structure had stood vacant for 2 years. There had been some vandalism and the swimming pool looked like a swamp. Two of the 13 central air-conditioning units were missing. Some doors and light fixtures were missing. But, the place was still beautiful and the potential was tremendous.

Our family stood silently in front of the building after the tour. Our daughters proclaimed the growing revelation we all sensed. "This is the Secret Place." Normally, a woman of vision, the enormity of the project weighed heavily on me. Our family was already challenged to believe God to meet our current monthly budget. And, that was with one air-conditioning unit. How could we ever believe God to pay for the electricity needed for thirteen air conditioners? However, the price of the facility reflected a distress situation. It would cost only 1/10 of its estimated value if fully restored. The vision was no longer for "someday."

In the ensuing days, I found myself arguing with God. This facility needed to go to someone who was more famous and had deeper pockets! I felt completely disqualified. But, He kept placing the demand. "Give me a drink." Now the test. Did I know the One who was asking? Was He faithful enough to perform His word? Was He able to use these unknown, empty-pocketed people?

When God makes a demand on your life, you will be miserable if you don't say "yes." So, with the sure knowledge we were in over our heads, we decided to give Him what He asked. Our obedience was the drink He requested from us. What God needs from you is always greater than anything you can give. Your vision and ability will always fall short of His vision for you. Only He can supply you with the ability to do what He needs.

Consider some of the situations you have read about in the newspapers. Faced with crisis situations, people required supernatural abilities to accomplish a task. Stories abound about people lifting cars after a wreck with supernatural strength to free a trapped infant or child.

What is even more amazing was how common, ordinary people faced extraordinary challenges and rose above their abilities when they trust God. The writer of Hebrews 11:32-40 tells their story:

And what more shall I say? For the time would fail me to tell of Gideon and Barak and Samson and Jephthah, also of David and Samuel and the prophets: who through faith subdued kingdoms, worked righteousness, obtained promises, stopped the mouths of lions, quenched the violence of fire, escaped the edge of the sword, out of weakness were made strong, became valiant in battle, turned to flight the armies of the aliens.

Women received their dead raised to life again. And others were tortured, not accepting deliverance, that they might obtain a better resurrection. Still others had trial of mockings and scourgings, yes, and of chains and imprisonment. They were stoned, they were sawn in two, were tempted, were slain with the sword.

*They wandered about in sheepskins and goatskins, being desti-
tute, afflicted, tormented—of whom the world was not worthy.
They wandered in deserts and mountains, in dens and caves of
the earth.*

*And all these, having obtained a good testimony through faith,
did not receive the promise, God having provided something better
for us, that they should not be made perfect apart from us.* (NKJ)

When athletes are challenged by the abilities of a superior athlete, they often rise above their own abilities to win the race, defeat the opponent or outlast the opposition. In the natural we see people make demands upon themselves that take them to greater levels. But in the supernatural, God invites and challenges us to make demands on him that stretch us far beyond our abilities so that we desperately cry out and demand His ability.

In responding to God's invitation regarding The Secret Place, the real question was not: *Did we have what it would take to accomplish this vision?* Of course, the supply for what we needed wasn't in us; it was in Him! So the real question was: *Did we know how to get whatever we needed to obey Him?*

We took the challenge. We placed a demand on the One who is able. Within three years, God sent us a core team of fifty servant-hearted people. Our meetings and conferences have filled every room to capacity. Even the new building we built for more people is overflowing. We moved to a big air-tent positioned on the tennis courts. Pastors and missionaries from all over the world come for refreshing, ministry and restoration. The facility houses a school of ministry, a mission organization, a network of ministries and our ministry offices.

Is God making a demand on your life right now? Have you resisted giving Him a drink because you feel disqualified? If you really know the One who has placed a demand, you will boldly ask for His presence to go with you. Whatever face you need, it is available to you. Even now, the Holy Spirit is already preparing you to get in position to turn to see the voice.

Chapter 4

Preparation To Make Your Demand

When John turned to see the voice, he was responding to a process that began in his life much earlier. Desperation will motivate us to turn. I was raised in an evangelical and strict atmosphere. My parents were sincere believers and faithful in their service to God.

When I was six years old, I had a genuine encounter with God. It was missions Sunday and a couple from Africa who were sponsored missionaries by our denomination were the guest speakers. Their joyful demeanor and enthusiasm drew me immediately. Usually sleepy, as soon as the preaching began, I was wide-awake and listening to every word.

They began to tell stories of the supernatural provision of God. While they were driving in the jungle one-day, they ran out of gas. They had no resources but the water of a stream nearby. With undaunted faith, they filled the gas tank with water. They believed that the same Jesus who could turn water into wine could turn water into gasoline! Amazingly, they continued on their journey without so much as one engine sputter.

They told another story about a tribe they had tried to reach with the Gospel to no avail. One day the chief and whole tribe showed up at their compound. The missionaries wanted to welcome their guests by preparing a meal. But, they only had one chicken and very little else. Knowing this opportunity must be seized, they prayed and asked God to cause one chicken to be enough to feed an entire village. They cooked it and began to serve their guests. Everyone ate their fill, God was glorified and the tribe received the Gospel. I was enraptured by their stories.

My six-year-old heart was captured by the possibilities of faith. Nothing was impossible! I made a decision that morning that I would not settle for less than the adventure I had just heard about. I had now entered the process of desperation that would compel me to a life of faith and miracles. Along the way, however, my desperation took a wrong turn.

Disillusioned with my search in the church for the kind of power I heard about on that missions Sunday, I looked elsewhere. There were many substitutes available. Everywhere I turned the world offered another option. I was drawn to the supernatural, but the church seemed devoid of supernatural power. The occult beckoned me with promises of doing well with the untapped power of my mind. I believed the lie that there are many roads to the same goal. Unfortunately, I bought it hook, line and sinker.

I am sad to report that the promises of supernatural activity were fulfilled. But, there are side effects of looking for God in the wrong place. I became an alcoholic by the time I was 14 years old. A spirit of fear tormented me night and day. My desperation was misguided. By the age of 17, I was diagnosed manic-depressive and agoraphobic.

A Wrong Turn Isn't The End

I rebelled as a teenager. My rebellion didn't end God's plan or destiny for my life. You may be heartbroken over your children's rebellion. You raised them in the church and did all you know to do. Yet, they seemed to have turned the wrong way. It may be that your children's hunger and desperation for the reality of a powerful God has taken a wrong turn. But, remember it's a process.

For me, my rebellion kept me from hearing God's voice for a season, but He didn't give up on me. Like the loving father of the prodigal son, God kept seeking me until I became desperate enough to return to His loving arms. In the words of a chorus we sing:

> *This is the air I breathe,*
> *This is the air I breathe,*
> *Your Holy Presence,*
> *Living in me.*
> *This is my daily bread,*
> *This is my daily bread,*
> *Your very word,*
> *Spoken to me.*
> *And I,*
> *I'm desperate for You.*
> *And I,*
> *I'm lost without You.*

Until we recognize we're desperate and lost, we'll not return to God's presence and word for our lives. Are you desperate to see His voice, to feel His Presence, and to be with Him?

Eventually, the effects of looking for the wrong voice created a new sense of desperation. My heart was crying out for help. Through a series of "coincidences," I encountered the supernatural God of my childhood. When I finally heard His voice, I turned to see His face and my life was changed. Desperation drove me to change my mind, my lifestyle and my heart's desires. God will sometimes allow you to have what you want so you can find out you don't want what you have. The process is God's way of preparation to cause us to turn to see His voice.

God's Restoring Love

The Bible story of Ruth and Naomi is a beautiful story of God's restoring love. The story begins with Elimelech, his wife Naomi and their two sons Mahlon and Chilion. Because there was famine in their hometown, Bethlehem, they decided to go to Moab to find provision. While in Moab both sons married women named Ruth and Orpah. Misfortune unfolded as Elimelech died and both sons followed him in death. Naomi was full of grief as she struggled to make ends meet with both daughters-in-law still in her household. The responsibility weighed heavily on Naomi and her disappointment brought her great distress.

In order to carry on the family name, it was the custom in their day for the son's widow to marry one of his brothers. In this case, it was impossible. There were no more sons. Naomi begged Ruth and Orpah to go back home. Orpah eventually agreed to return home as Naomi had requested. Ruth, however, was another matter. Ruth viewed herself as a true daughter and would not leave Naomi's side. She swore allegiance to Naomi and the God of her fathers. These two women went back to Bethlehem and began to establish their home.

Because they had no husband or harvest fields, Ruth went out to a relative's wheat field and began to glean the leftovers in the fields after the reapers were finished. The relative, Boaz, noticed Ruth in the field. He was favorably impressed. In fact, he told his reapers to drop some of their good harvest in her path so she would get more than leftovers. When Ruth returned home, Naomi realized what was happening. This relative could be the kinsman redeemer she needed to give security to Ruth and herself. It was the custom that when there were no more sons, the closest male relative takes the widow as his wife.

However, there was a problem. Boaz was not the closest make relative. So, Naomi put a plan in motion to make a demand on Boaz to become Ruth's kinsman redeemer in Ruth 3:1-4:

> One day Naomi her mother-in-law said to her, "My daughter, should I not try to find a home for you, where you will be well provided for? Is not Boaz, with whose servant girls you have been,

a kinsman of ours? Tonight he will be winnowing barley on the threshing floor. Wash and perfume yourself, and put on your best clothes. Then go down to the threshing floor, but don't let him know you are there until he has finished eating and drinking. When he lies down, note the place where he is lying. Then go and uncover his feet and lie down. He will tell you what to do.

Upon closer examination, there is a very methodical preparation required of Ruth. Her first instruction was to wash herself. Ruth had been in the field all day with the workers. She was dirty from her labor and smelled like a working slave. The first thing she had to do was wash off all the accumulated filth of where she had been. She could not present herself to Boaz still reeking of the stench of the past.

Many of us try to approach God with the stale aroma of our past. The aroma of the "old thing" is a stench in God's nostrils. Washing changed her status from field hand to bride. Washing ourselves in the water of His word helps us to change our status. No longer a slave to the bondage of the past, we can approach our Redeemer with confidence.

But, aren't we already cleansed from sin by the blood of Jesus? Absolutely! We have been washed in the blood. That washing cleanses us from the sin that will send us into eternity without God. But there are thought and behavior patterns that must be changed. Washing by the water of the Word renews our mind and helps us to break off the yoke of the old pattern in our behavior.

The old man (read 2 Corinthians 5:17) seeks to gain preeminence while the new man learns to put down everything that exalts itself against the knowledge of God. If we do not wash ourselves in the renewing water, we could have a great destiny and still live like a slave.

Unworthiness is not humility. Some of us have operated so long under the yoke of unworthiness that we think it is humility. Humility is the attitude of a servant's heart. There is a difference between a servant and a slave. The servant chooses, the slave has no choice. It's the difference between obedience and submission. A slave obeys, a servant submits.

Our girls were so close in age that they sometimes bickered over silly things. As parents, we wanted them to get along so we would make them apologize and give each other a hug. No matter how much we tried to instill the importance of loving one another with the right attitude, the atmosphere was so frosty you thought a northern wind had blown in. They obeyed, but they didn't submit. Thank God for those other rare moments when they didn't know we were looking. They would hold hands and play or give each other a spontaneous hug. Our Father wants us to approach Him as a willing and loving servant, not a commanded slave.

Unworthiness leads to jealousy. If we operate as an unworthy child, we will get jealous of the liberty in our brothers and sisters.

If we deem ourselves unworthy, we will judge others to be unworthy too.

Set aside your pride. We must wash ourselves from the aroma of laboring in the fields. Our approach to God must be unencumbered from the works of the flesh. We cannot make a demand on His presence with a spirit of pride.

Sometimes our attitude is, "Look what I've done. Look who I am." In the presence of the LORD there is only one superstar! Our confidence must be in Him alone, never in our own ability.

Leaders, we must be very careful. If we continue to labor as we approach God, we will lead others into that lifestyle. The vision must not become a work of flesh. We must strive to enter the rest of God's kingdom. Works can puff you up or wear you out. Some of us are unable to approach God because we're just too tired to make the effort!

Wash Away the Past and Your Pride

Our Christian walk in the Spirit is not about doing; it's about being in relationship with God. That relationship requires purity and holiness, not good works. Our efforts flow out of a joyful service to Christ not the desire to be approved because of our hard work or effort.

We are priests of the most high God. Peter writes, "But you are a chosen people, a royal priesthood..." (1 Peter 2:9). Priests do not enter God's presence by the sweat of hard work. In fact, wearing anything that causes a priest to sweat is prohibited in Ezekiel 44:18, "They shall have linen turbans on their heads and linen trousers on their bodies; they shall not clothe themselves with anything that causes sweat."

We must wash and purify ourselves from every labor and effort that we produce trying to gain entry into His Presence that we might see His voice. Not only are we saved by grace, not by works (Eph. 2:8), we also walk by grace not by works. Our faith in Christ produces good fruit or works not the opposite. Good work doesn't produce faith or grace. Stop sweating your way into His presence. The most sweat will ever produce is smelly pride which is a stale aroma to God and those around us. Wash yourself clean from the sweat of pride.

Anoint Yourself in His Aroma

After Ruth washed, she was instructed to anoint herself. She had to wash herself first or she would have anointed the "old thing." She could have tried to cover the stench of her day in the field by applying lots of perfume. But the old smell is undeniable. It's like squirting a spray air-freshener in a room where people are smoking cigars. The mixture is worse than the original smell. There are many in the body of Christ trying to spray a little perfume on the old and present it as a new thing. If you miss the first step of washing, you can present only a mixture.

We have been training leaders for many years. People with a

call of God on their lives are usually anxious to move ahead as quickly as possible into their purpose. They always think they are ready before they are. The anointing can be a dangerous thing. It can make you think you are something you are not. So, God requires us to go through the process of washing and renewing. Like Namaan the word of the LORD comes to us, "Wash yourself!" (2 Kings 5:10)

Promotion Comes by Character and Preparation Not Gifting. There are many, however, who do take the shortcut. In our celebrity-driven atmosphere, we tend to promote people by gifting, rather then character or preparation. Several years ago, I was responsible for a conference. I came into contact with a minister who had a powerful testimony. He had been a Hollywood personality who was gloriously saved. We all rejoiced at his salvation. He was already on the television circuit and ministering in conferences. I asked him to come minister at our conference. We were thrilled when he said "yes."

As the day approached, we were becoming increasingly concerned with the advance communication. The flight arrangements were not good enough, so we had to buy new tickets on the preferred airline. We were asked, "Could you please hire a professional photographer to take pictures of the ministry?" There were other demands that were excessive. As a traveling minister for nearly 20 years, I certainly have an understanding about communicating your needs.

Being on the road is an exercise in endurance and patience. Most of the time, your hosts are thoughtful and do their best to meet your needs. But, there are those occasional horror stories that make you question your call to traveling ministry. So, I could understand some of his requests. We did our best to meet his needs. However, by the time the conference was over, this man's star had begun to tarnish. He railed over our not picking him up in a limousine at the airport. He was offended that I wanted him to meet before the service to go over the details of the meeting. His testimony was powerful. His character was sadly lacking.

I learned a BIG lesson that weekend. There is a rich depth of ministry that flows from a life broken and submitted through the process of holiness. **We have to stop anointing the mixture.**

We oversee a network of ministers and churches. Part of our responsibility is to oversee the licensing and ordination process. We must be in tune with God's voice to know His timing. When we first started the network, we ordained ministers we had known by years of relationship. As the network grew, we received applications from people with whom we had very little relationship. The Holy Spirit gave me a warning in the process of considering applications. The scripture says in 1 Timothy 5:22 that we should not lay hands upon anyone too hastily and thus share responsibility for the sins of others…"

The Holy Spirit told me that if I laid hands on ministers in which I did not have a proven relationship, I could put them in premature warfare that could destroy them. Every new level of authority that is released in our lives will bring a new level of warfare. David was wise enough to fight Goliath in his own clothes with the weapons that had already been proven in his life. Even though he would be king someday, it wasn't time yet for him to put on the king's armor.

God's anointing produces a sweet aroma. When Ruth was instructed to anoint herself, she was really being instructed to put on a fresh aroma. We believers are to be a sweet aroma to Him as we read in 2 Corinthians 2:14-15: "But thanks be to God, who always leads us in His triumph in Christ, and manifests through us the sweet aroma of the knowledge of Him in every place. For we are a fragrance of Christ to God among those who are being saved and among those who are perishing...."

My husband Steve and I have been married over 30 years. I have known him since I was 13 years old. Because we love each other, we want to please one another. There are certain types of cologne I want him to wear. Likewise, he has a favorite perfume he wants me to wear. When we are close, I recognize the familiar aroma of his cologne. In fact, sometimes, when I lay my head on his pillow, I know he has been there because I can smell the fragrance of his cologne. But, I'm the only one who gets close enough to smell his pillow! Only those intimately involved with Father get close enough to partake of His aroma.

The reality is that in order to anoint ourselves, we must press in for a face-to-face encounter. If we linger long enough in the aroma of His presence, the residual fragrance will be upon our lives. To anoint ourselves we must partake of the anointing of His presence. In the early church, the apostles were marked by the anointing of "having been with Jesus" (Acts 4:13). Everywhere they went, the aroma of Jesus' anointing lingered on their walk, their talk, and their every action. Do others smell the sweet perfume of Jesus' presence on you when they are with you? Do they immediately know that you have been with Jesus?

After washing and anointing herself, Ruth was instructed to put on a new garment. In order to approach Boaz as a bride, she had to lay aside the clothes of a slave and put on a clean garment. She had to take off the old and put on the new. The process of preparation requires us to "put on" after we have "taken off." This part of the process is the key to walking in victory.

We are a people who have learned how to put off the old man, but we often fail in putting on the new man. We have become very deliverance-minded. Our desire is to get free from bondage. It is commendable to want to be delivered. However, the deliverance will not bring permanent victory unless we have learned to put on. The children of Israel were brought out of Egypt by God's mighty arm of power. Israel was brought out of Egypt (Ps. 136:11) for the purpose of being brought into the promised land (Joshua 1).

You are delivered from bondage to your destiny. Even as

God was delivering them FROM bondage, He was delivering them TO their destiny. They did not understand the necessity to put off Egypt and put on the promise. They were continually struggling because they had not changed their identity or perception of themselves. When Moses sent the spies into the Promised Land, they encountered giants. Because the Israelites had not put on their new victor's garments, they still perceived themselves as victims. Therefore, the giants perceived them as victims. "There we saw the giants…and we were like grasshoppers in our own sight, and so we were in their sight" Num.13:33.

The ten intimidated spies saw themselves as victims not victors. They were wimps not warriors. As a result, they swayed an entire generation of Israelites to flee from God's promise and destiny. They chose to wander in a wilderness only miles away from the promise rather than to go in and possess the land. That entire generation had to die with the except of Joshua and Caleb.

The ten spies had a spirit of rejection that produced that same spirit in an entire people. The same can happen in any church. The fearful and timid can infect an entire people keeping them from God's vision, purpose and destiny. God calls us to be strong and very courageous in order to step into the promised land (Josh. 1). The early disciples were marked by boldness (Acts 4:13). Reject rejection and embrace the courage to obey God's voice and enter into your destiny.

When we are born again, we are brought out of darkness and

brought into His marvelous light. The Bible says we have been sanctified and set apart. We view sanctification as the process of being separated from the old, but it means more than that alone. Even as we are being set apart from the bondage, we are being set apart for the purposes of God.

God heals us so that we can be a healer. He delivers us so that we can be deliverers. This truth is often lacking in the lives of those who chronically deal with the same old issues. The perception of who they are never changes. There is a continual search for freedom by coming out of bondage. But, coming out is only the beginning of the process.

Put on a Fresh Garment

Even if you are washed and anointed by His presence, you must put on a fresh garment. It is necessary for the purposes of God to be activated in your life. The alcoholic must put on the garment of sobriety. The abused victim must be clothed in a victor mentality. The anointing of His presence will compel you to commissioning and purpose.

In Isaiah 6, Isaiah perceived himself correctly as a man of unclean lips. At the altar of fire, he was cleansed with the coal. He was delivered from the bondage of his sin. But, God wasn't through with him. In verse 9 we read, "And He said, 'Go, and tell this people...'"

Thank God for the anointing that breaks the yoke of oppression. But, being set free does not guarantee you will remain free. You know what I am talking about. How many times have we been to the altar and received a real touch from God only to find ourselves in need of deliverance again at the next altar service? The process of washing and anointing must be followed by putting on a new garment.

When Ruth was preparing to meet with Boaz, she could not go to him clothed in the old garments. She was being transformed and her status was changing. She was no longer the poor relative who gleaned the leftovers in his field. She was now the unfulfilled bride preparing to make a demand on the inheritance she could rightfully pursue.

Wait for the Right Moment

There was another step in the process of preparation. Washed, anointed and appropriately clothed, Ruth was instructed to go down to the threshing floor and wait for the right moment. The threshing floor was the place where the barley harvest was laid on the floor and the oxen threshed it by stomping on the outer shell in order to release the barley grain inside. After the oxen had trodden on the barley, it was picked up on a tray and taken outside. The threshed barley was thrown into the air. The chaff (the old hard shell) would be carried by the wind. The barley kernel would fall back onto the tray. So, the threshing floor was the process of releasing the edible seed from the outer shell.

The threshing floor was the house of refining. Even though Ruth had walked faithfully through the preparation, she still had to go to the house of refinement. Refining is never easy. The fire is hot and the process can be jarring, but it is necessary if we want to release seed of potential out of our hard, outer shell.

Ruth was instructed to go to the threshing floor and wait for the right time to approach Boaz. After he had relaxed and eaten, Ruth was to go lay down at the foot of his bed and uncover his feet. After she obeyed Naomi's instructions, Ruth waited at his feet. When the chill of the night air made his feet cold, Boaz was startled awake. He realized a woman was at his feet and he asked her to identify herself. Her response tells the whole story. ["And he said, "Who are you?" And she answered, "I am Ruth your maid. So spread your covering over your maid, for you are a close relative" (Ruth 3:9).]

Make a Demand at the Right Time

Ruth was prepared and ready to make her demand. She said, "Cover me with your cloak." In their custom, when a man covered a woman with his cloak, it was a symbol of their commitment to be husband and wife. When Boaz asked her to identify herself, she could have answered in a way that he would understand. She could have said, "I am Ruth, the daughter-in-law of Naomi, who gleans in your fields." But, she had already washed off the sweat of the field, she had already anointed herself and she had already put on new clothes. She was no longer the beggar. She was asking for what belonged to her. She had confidence in the preparation process so that she could boldly make her claim.

Boaz's response is somewhat surprising. I don't know about you, but if somebody uncovered my feet while I was sleeping and caused me to be startled awake, I would not be a happy camper! In fact, he was pleased beyond measure that she had approached him so boldly. The end result of her action is that Boaz called her a virtuous woman and made her his wife. Ruth proved that the diligent seeker will be rewarded.

Virtue arises out of righteous boldness. Virtue in Hebrew means forceful or strong. It is the same word used in Proverbs 31 in describing a virtuous woman. Ruth was qualified as virtuous by:

1. She made herself a daughter even against Naomi's wishes. Just like Elisha made a bold demand on Elijah, Ruth made a demand. Elijah told Elisha to leave him, but Elisha made himself a true son instead of an assistant. He made a demand on Elijah.
2. Ruth worked faithfully through the process.
3. Ruth could have chosen a more desirable, younger man, but she made her demand on the right man. When we finally become frustrated with people's failures to satisfy us, we will become desperate and make a demand on the right man—Jesus himself.

The scriptural precedent is clear. Our desperation to see the Voice will cause us to make a bold claim on His presence. That same desperation will give us the motivation we need to endure the process required. With the invitation of God Himself and the help of the Holy Spirit, we must walk boldly into the throne of grace and find our help in time of trouble.

Do you remember the story of the missionaries whom God used to stir my faith when I was just six years old? Their stories of God's miraculous intervention started me on my desperate journey to see His voice. I never forgot them or the miracles they shared. When Steve and I were born again nearly 20 years later the impact of their lives remained. Just two months after we came to the Lord, we had the opportunity to take a trailer of clothes and food to Mexico. We lived in Texas, so it was approximately a ten-hour drive to the border. We were so in love with Jesus, we jumped at the chance to do something for him.

We really did not have the money or the wisdom to strike out across the country. But, we did have child-like faith. As we traveled down a long stretch of lonely road with no civilization for several hours, we ran out of gas. There was no hope or service stations in sight when I remembered the missionaries. I quickly told Steve and we got some water out of the ditch next to the road. After we laid hands on the gas tank, we started the car and went on to our destination.

We had made a demand on the power and presence of God.

He responded not because we were deserving, worthy or had earned it. But like Ruth, we had a holy boldness resulting from being:

1) Washed and purified from the past and pride.

2) Anointed by the sweet aroma of Jesus' presence.

3) Clothed in the fresh garment of a new creation in Christ.

4) In the right place having waited for the right time to make a demand on His promise and presence in our lives.

Are you ready to walk in such boldness? Are you desperate to see His voice?

The presence of God is available and free. But, His presence is not cheap. David learned that making a demand on the presence of God could be costly if not done God's way. Be bold, be strong – but be very careful!

Chapter 5

Carriers or Handlers

Mecca is the holy city of promise for millions of Islamic believers. The supreme goal of every true Muslim is to make a pilgrimage at some moment in their lives. During a recent holy festival 2,000,000 followers were pressing in to the holy city as many were realizing their life-long dream. In their desperate attempt to fulfill their heart's desire, they began to run toward their sacred shrine. Many people who could not keep up with the crowd were pushed down only to be trampled to death by the throngs of worshippers. The fervor of their devotion was commendable, but their desperation caused others to lose their lives.

When people burn with misplaced passion, destruction can be the result. Just having good intention is not enough. **We must define the difference between desperation and carnally motivated pursuit.**

Several years ago I was invited to minister in a Texas church. At that time I was a minister who also moved in the prophetic realm. I gained a reputation for ministering personal prophecy for several hours in every meeting. Many times, I ministered prophetically to every person in attendance. I labored under a misconception that if I could do it I should do it. Before I came into a meeting or started a revival, the pastors would tell me their congregation was hungry to hear from God.

Often the pastor would introduce me by saying something like the following, "We are so pleased to have Sister Shirley Arnold with us. I know the LORD has sent her to bring us a word from the Lord. If you need a personal word from the Lord, she will minister to each one of you." You can imagine the pressure I felt all the time. After all, people had fasted and prayed while waiting for me to bring them a word from God!

The Texas church was no exception. After several hours of ministry, we made our way back to the hotel. I was exhausted and feeling strange. Although the ministry had been extremely powerful and accurate, I felt used and empty. As I sat on the edge of that hotel bed, the Spirit of God spoke to me. **He told me that I had to learn the difference between need and greed.**

What some people call hunger is nothing more than their attempt to be touched by God without paying the price to pursue God themselves. From that moment forward, I was released from the pressure of answering man's greed. As we pursue God and His presence, our motives will be examined. Good intentions are not enough. Ungoverned passion can have deadly results.

Passion for God's Presence

King David was passionate in his resolve to restore the presence of the LORD back to Israel. The ark of the convenant had fallen into enemy hands during a battle at Ebenezar with the Philistines in 1 Samuel 4. Israel had a good idea—bring the ark into battle to insure a victory. But man's good idea isn't a God idea. Religious passion never brings spiritual victory. During their losing battle to the Philistines, they tried to use the presence of the LORD without seeking His direction.

We must continue to submit ourselves to the government of God even when our intentions are zealous, because our our intent can be evil (Zech. 1:13-15). Israel did not seek God's order for the battle; so the enemy captured the ark of God's presence and set it in their temple alongside their own idols.

Interestingly enough, the idols of the Philistines could not stand next to the ark. Each time the idols toppled, the priests tried to pick up their idols and put them back into place. No human effort can make an idol stand. In fact, the Dagon idols even lost their heads. It became apparent to the priests that the God of the Israelites was much more powerful than their own gods.

But Jehovah was not finished with His show of power. The people began to experience the physical plague of hemorrhoids. The whole nation was suffering because the Ark of the Covenant was in their possession. They concluded that the only way to relief would be to send the ark to Israel. So, they got a new cart, placed the ark on it along with a trespass offering.

The oxen drew the cart to the countryside of Beth-Shemesh. The Israelite men who discovered the cart were so excited, they touched the ark and many unfortunately died. The ark was then transferred to the house of Abinadah where it remained for many years during the reign of Saul.

When David became king, there was a national revival of patriotism and religious fervor. King David was consumed with the presence of the LORD and a desire to bring the ark to the city of David.

> So David assembled all Israel together, from the Shihor of Egypt even to the entrance of Hamath, to bring the ark of God from Kiriath-jearim. And David and all Israel went up to Baalah, that is, to Kiriath-jearim, which belongs to Judah, to bring up from there the ark of God, the LORD who is enthroned above the cherubim, where His name is called. And they carried the ark of God on a new cart from the house of Abinadab, and Uzza and Ahio drove the cart. And David and all Israel were celebrating before God with all their might, even with songs and with lyres, harps, tambourines, cymbals, and with trumpets. When they came to the threshing floor of Chidon, Uzza put out his hand to hold the ark, because the oxen nearly upset it. And the anger of the LORD burned against Uzza, so He struck him down because he put out his hand to the ark; and he died there before God. (1 Chronicles 13: 5-10)

The result of this well-intentioned endeavor was destruction. King David was devastated. In the midst of all the celebration, Uzza met his death. How could this happen? Upon closer examination, it makes more sense. Uzza was of the order of the Kohathite. As one of the three branches of the Levitical priesthood, God had instructed them very specifically concerning their priestly duties.

"And when Aaron and his sons have finished covering the holy objects and all the furnishings of the sanctuary, when the camp is to set out, after that the sons of Kohath shall come to carry the, so that they may not touch the holy objects and die. These are the things in the tent of meetings which the sons of Kohath are to carry" (Numbers 4:15).

From the beginning, God had made it clear that the sons of Kohath were not to touch the ark under any circumstances. From generation to generation, they were warned of the death penalty they would receive if they violated God's order. The following passage deserves the distinction between the three orders of priesthood.

> *"Two carts and four oxen he gave to the son of Gershon, according to their service, and four carts and eight oxen he gave to the sons of Merari, according to their service, under the direction of Ithamar the son of Aaron the priest.* **But he did not give any to the sons of Kohath because theirs was the service of the holy objects, which they carried on the shoulder**" (Numbers 7:7-9).

The Gershonites and the Merari ranks were given the use of oxen and carts. But the Kohathites were not allowed to even own a cart or oxen. Their primary responsibility was to carry the ark on staves upon their shoulders.

They should never have handled the ark. Their job was to carry the presence of the Lord. The nature of their responsibility would require them to stoop low to position themselves to carry the ark. But, they violated several important principles.

1. God means what He says!
2. There is no good substitute for God's order!
3. Don't put your hands on it!
4. Good intentions are not good enough!

God Means What He Says!

I have to admit that Uzza's death seemed rather extreme to me. However, the word of God was very clear. Isn't it amazing how often we think we are the exception? Without the fear of the Lord, we will begin to add or subtract from the word of the Lord.

There is a very sad pattern in families I have observed throughout the body of Christ. The children of believers seem to be the least well behaved. Children resist boundaries and do not respect authority. You can ask any pastor and they will tell you the same thing. Children have no regard for property or rules.

How can this be? There are many societal influences we could elaborate upon like one-parent families, both parents working, the general attitude of disrespect in the media, etc. But, the glaring truth is that many children do not respect authority for two reasons. (1) Children figure out quickly that parents don't mean what they say because they don't follow through consistently with discipline and, (2) children observe their own parent's behavior regarding authority.

A child who has not learned there are consequences to his or her actions will never respect authority. We harm our own children and eventually the society they live in when we allow them to set their own boundaries. A look at the newspaper will quickly validate this sad conclusion. Children are murdering other children and their teachers in school – an institute that should stand as a place of authority. Just making rules will not solve the problems. **There must be a price to pay for violating the rules.**

Unfortunately, too many parents have abdicated their role of authority in the home to become just a "friend" of their kids. It only complicates the issues when our children observe how we relate to authority. The lack of respect for all authority including spiritual authority only seems to support the erosion of the fear of the Lord.

There's No Substitute for God's Order

How many churches have you attended in the last 10 years? Do you leave the church when you don't agree with the pastor or leadership? Do you talk negatively about those who are in authority in your life? (That list would include your employer, government officials and spiritual leaders). When my husband and I began to pastor a church, it was quite an eye-opening experience. The LORD told us to offer membership because we live in a society that is transient and people needed a place to belong. Because so many have never put down roots anywhere, we suffer from a lack of commitment and covenant relationship.

To our great surprise, the first exodus out of the church came when we announced that we would be receiving members. We were accused of being controlling and restrictive. People used the scripture, "where the Spirit of the LORD is, there is liberty" to support their misguided position of freedom.

The lack of respect for spiritual authority has had a more deadly effect. Our disregard for discipline and commitment to truth causes us to rationalize the very word of God. Somehow, we have come to believe we are the exception to God's rules. A well-known minister in recent times was known for His fiery holiness messages that came against sexual impurity. In public, he was the voice of outrage against pornography and immorality. However, in his private life, he continued to indulge his carnal lust with those very things. When he was discovered in his sin, we all felt the pain.

How could he continue day after day practicing the very thing he preached against? I have no doubt that this man was a genuine lover of God who desired to be free from his sin. However, God means what he says. **As you cry out for all of Him, He will come for all of you!**

When God gave Moses the plan for the Tabernacle, He told Moses to be very careful to do exactly as he was instructed. Hebrews 8 says the Tabernacle was a type and a shadow of that which was to come. In other words, the details are important to God. As we read in Hebrews 8:5, "who serve a copy and shadow of the heavenly things, just as Moses was warned by God when he was about to erect the tabernacle; for, See, He says, that you make all things according to the pattern which was shown you on the mountain."

God has a pattern or order that he has established in every realm. When the Holy Spirit hovered over the darkness and chaos of the deep in Genesis 1:2, God was bringing order in the earth. He said, "let there be light"and the formless void and darkness took shape.

So, God had given David His order for bringing in the presence of the Lord. Good intentions surrounded the whole event. The atmosphere was filled with praise and anticipation. Surely, a few, small details would not be important. After all, the most important thing was bringing the ark to the city of David. Did it really matter how it happened? Didn't the *end justify the means*? The answer to those questions became painfully obvious.

Don't Put Your Hands on It!

When the oxen stumbled, it was only natural to reach out and steady the ark. It seemed a noble response to the situation. Of course, if God's directions had been followed from the beginning, there would have been no cart or oxen to stumble. Therefore, there would have been no need for Uzza to put out his hand. If Uzza had been in proper position, he would have been a carrier of the presence instead of a handler. The holy thing was treated in a common way. Perhaps he had become too familiar with the ark while it had resided in Abinadab's house.

At times, we become too familiar with the things of God and even God Himself. We enjoy ourselves regularly in worship until we take God's presence in worship for granted. We experience answered prayer often and so we come to expect God to speak to us in familiar ways. But how does flesh ever become completely familiar with Spirit. Certainly holiness must inspire awe, mystery and the fear of the Lord. We must always receive the presence of God with reverence, not familiarity.

You might be thinking, "Wait a minute. Father invites us to come boldly into the throneroom when we have a need!" What a precious privilege it is to know we have immediate and instant access to the presence of the Lord. But, never forget it is still HIS throneroom. That means, we are invited to the place of His government. When we come to Him, we should never forget who is in charge.

I never ceased to be amazed at the availability of God to His people. In meeting after meeting, the presence of the LORD is overwhelming. We have seen powerful miracles with many manifestations of God in our midst. But, sometimes I wonder if we have become too familiar with His presence. Have we been touched so many times that we no longer thrill to His touch? I see more people daring God for a blessing than getting into position to seek His face.

Elijah's servant was sent to look at the sky for a sign after his confrontation with the prophets of Baal. Fire had fallen from heaven and the children of Israel had declared their allegiance to Jehovah God. When the servant took his first look, he saw a cloud the size of a man's hand. When he reported his findings to Elijah the prophet sent him back to look again.

After returning seven times, the servant returned with a report of a heavy shower. Elijah was not willing to settle for a cloud the size of a man's hand. He pressed in until he received the rain of heaven.

Many Christians have never seen the heavy shower of God's presence. They have only experienced the amount of rain that comes from a cloud of the size of a man's hand. We have settled for the overflow of someone else's anointing instead of pressing through to wait for a revelation that comes from God Himself.

One disturbing tendency seems to be evident in every move of God. The beginnings are marked by the lack of man's involvement. God sovereignly shows up and the people are awe struck. Slowly but surely, man begins to put his hands on it. **They become handlers instead of carriers.**

Good Intentions are Not Enough

Bringing the ark into the city was a good idea. The nation Israel was excited about the event. There was dancing, singing, and celebration. With this much good intention, surely nothing could go wrong. You can imagine King David's reaction when Uzza died.

As painful as this lesson turned out to be, it caused David to examine his heart and his motives. For the next three months, he waited on the Lord. David knew the will of God. He simply did not follow the way of God. After three months of seeking the Lord, he called for the Levitical priesthood and prepared to carry the presence of the LORD into the city in proper order.

Again, the singing, dancing, and celebration were in place. However this time the processional stopped every seven steps to build an altar and make offering. The handlers became carriers and the people stopped often to humble themselves before the Lord.

If you have a desire to see God, your journey must be marked by humility. God resists prideful hearts, but He draws near to the humble heart.

Ask yourself:

- Do I really believe that God means what He says!
- Have I eliminated every substitute for God's order!
- Am I refusing to touch God's glory?
- Do I understand that good intentions are not good enough?
- Have I humbly submitted to God in being a carrier and not a handler of His presence?

Chapter 6

Seeing His Voice

W hen John turned to see the voice, he could never have imagined what his eyes would behold. The Apostle John had walked and talked with Jesus during his 3-year ministry on earth. On a daily basis he observed Jesus and could surely have described his LORD in great detail. But, when John turned to see the voice, he saw Jesus as he had never seen him before.

> *And I turned to see the voice that was speaking with me. And having turned I saw seven golden lampstands; and in the middle of the lampstands one like a son of man, clothed in a robe reaching to the feet, and girded across His breast with a golden girdle.*
>
> *And His head and His hair were white like white wool, like snow; and His eyes were like a flame of fire; and His feet {were} like burnished bronze, when it has been caused to glow in a furnace, and His voice {was} like the sound of many waters.*
>
> *And in His right hand He held seven stars; and out of His mouth came a sharp two-edged sword; and His face was like the sun shining in its strength.* (Rev. 1:12-16 NAS)

John was awestruck by the glory he experienced in this new revelation of Jesus. In fact, he became afraid and fell like a dead man at the feet of Jesus.

If John had not made a demand on the voice he heard, he would have known Jesus only by his past revelation. We must not be afraid of seeing our God in all the facets of who He really is. Most of us seek the face of a God we recognize. We want Him to look like we have pictured Him. Our revelation of God is generally limited to our needs. We love the revelation of the provider, the healer and the deliverer. However, this God that we love is so much more.

One day in worship, I began to cry out to the Lord, "I want to see your face." His immediate response was, "You don't really want to see my face. You want to see the face of the One you recognize." If you are a desperate seeker, you must be prepared for the multi-faceted revelation of our God.

When Moses was in the desert after killing the Egyptian, he turned aside to see God as a burning bush.

> And the angel of the LORD appeared to him in a blazing fire from the midst of a bush; and he looked, and behold, the bush was burning with fire, yet the bush was not consumed.
>
> So Moses said, "I must turn aside now, and see this marvelous sight, why the bush is not burned up." When the LORD saw that he turned aside to look, God called to him from the midst of the bush, and said, "Moses, Moses!" And he said, "Here I am."
>
> Then He said, "Do not come near here; remove your sandals from your feet, for the place on which you are standing is holy

ground." He said also, "I am the God of your father, the God of Abraham, the God of Isaac, and the God of Jacob." Then Moses hid his face, for he was afraid to look at God. (Exodus 3:2-6 NAS)

In Old Testament scripture, whenever God revealed Himself in a direct, visible manifestation, it is called a *theophany*. While a person does not actually see God Himself, he does see the immediate effects of God's unmediated presence. Frequently the visible presence of God is called the "Angel of the Lord." So the pillar of cloud by day and fire by night (Ex. 13:21-22, and the pillar of fire and cloud at Mt. Sinai (Ex. 24:16-18), and the shekinah cloud of God's glory (Ex. 40:34-38) are all theophanies. The startling manifestations of God's presence always seem to bring awe, wonder, and bring us face to face with powerful new revelation.

The face of God is not white, black, red or yellow. It is not young or old, male or female. He is not exclusively any of these descriptions and yet, He is all of them. Let me ask you:

- Have you limited God to a face you recognize?
- Do you feel safe in keeping Him limited to the face that fulfills your needs?

There seems to be a pattern in the process of God revealing

Himself to those who make a demand on His presence. The focus changes from the seeker's need to God's agenda. For example:

- When Moses turned to see the burning bush, he was given the responsibility to deliver his people from bondage (Exodus 3).
- When Isaiah saw the LORD as high and lifted up, he was commissioned to take the word of judgment to His people (Isaiah 6).
- When John turned to see the voice, he was commanded to write down and deliver the revelation of Jesus Christ to the church. God trusts those who are willing to see Him as He really is (Revelation 1).

Going Higher to a New Perspective

After John received the letters to send to the churches, he continued to look. "After these things I looked, and behold, a door {standing} open in heaven, and the first voice which I had heard, like {the sound} of a trumpet speaking with me, said, "Come up here, and I will show you what must take place after these things" (Rev. 4:1 NAS).

John was invited to a higher revelation of the Lord. In Philippians 3, Paul described it as the "upward call of Christ Jesus." When you turn to see the voice, you will always be challenged to come up higher. Why? Because your perspective will change. You will begin to see from God's vantage point.

I was in a rural part of our nation driving through miles and miles of farmland. Everywhere I looked, there was another field of corn or beans or wheat. Actually, it was quite boring after a while, because it all looked the same. After ministering in several churches, it was time for me to fly home. When the airplane took off, I was mesmerized by the sight below. Those farmlands became a patchwork quilt of colors and shapes. It was breathtaking. Those same boring farmlands had become a beautiful, intricately designed collage like a piece of artwork.

What had changed? My perspective. When I came up higher, I changed perspective. I could now see the big picture. Being lifted up out of the earthbound perspective gave me a fuller understanding. In order to gain God's perspective, you must be willing to answer that upward call. And, it doesn't come cheap.

If you like just being a part of the crowd, you will never step up to God's perspective. When you start to see things from God's viewpoint, you will lose your place in the crowd. Moses sent 12 spies into the Promised Land to get their report. Ten of those spies looked at the giants in that land and quickly adopted an earthbound perspective. In fact, they saw themselves like grasshoppers in their own eyes. Therefore, the giants began to view them the same way.

But Joshua and Caleb had a completely different reaction.

While 10 spies were looking up at the giants, these 2 men were looking down on the promise. The whole congregation was against them. They even wanted to stone them. Multitude mentality will always rob you of the higher vision. You can no longer hide in the crowd when you gain God's perspective. Like Paul, you will see the open door for effective service instead of the adversaries who oppose you. **You become proactive instead of reactive.**

A Higher Call Leads to Action

The call to come higher will lead you to take action. David went to the front lines of battle to take cheese and bread to his brothers. When David arrived at the battle lines, he was very confused. What had happened to the mighty armies of Israel? They were cowering under the threats of one Philistine name Goliath. Apparently, the day to day realities of battle had stripped Israel of their vision. All they could see and hear were the threats of their enemy.

Clothed in their armor, they went out every day to battle, but they returned every night in defeat. They were paralyzed by the circumstances.

When David observed what was going on, he was angry at the enemy's advantage. After all, the same God who had enabled him to kill a lion and a bear threatening his sheep was the same God with him against this "uncircumcised Philistine." *Moved to action,* this young shepherd boy brought down the mighty Goliath with a slingshot and five smooth stones. He was *moved to action* by the revelation of God's ability over the weakness of man held in bondage to an earthbound perspective.

When we become paralyzed by our circumstances, we need to come higher. If the enemy can defeat you with fear, he has already won the battle. But when you begin to see things from God's perspective, you will be moved to action.

The View From God's Perspective

God's perspective always brings in the new. God chides us, "Forget the former things; do not dwell on the past. See, I am doing a new thing! Now it springs up; do you not perceive it? (Isa. 43:18-19). Before we come up higher, we are mired in the bog of past defeats, limited visions, and broken dreams. The old perspective can only reveal what we lacked and where we fell short. But God has a new perspective for us from above. Remember: *we have been raised up with Christ to sit with Him in heavenly places* (Eph. 2:6).

Taking position in God's perspective will cause you to see what you have instead of what you don't have. Elisha and his servant were surrounded by the Syrian armies. They were angry with the prophet who knew their military strategy through supernatural means. Elijah warned the king of Israel many times of the Syrian battle plan. When Elisha's servant saw the Syrian armies, he panicked. All he could see from his earthbound perspective was the enemy's show of strength.

Elisha was not moved at all. He had gained the higher revelation, a new perspective. For the servant's sake, Elisha prayed for the LORD to show the true picture. In a flash, the servant's eyes were opened to see the armies of the hosts of heaven. Their horses and chariots of fire surrounded Elisha. The servant had been under a false perception. Without coming up higher, he would have never seen who was for him, instead of who was against him.

Those who operate in earthbound perspective consider their own inabilities like the 10 spies. Earthbound people will look at natural resources like Elisha's servant and they lose their passion for action like the armies of Israel. But, those who come up higher into the realm of God's perspective will keep their eyes on the vision like Caleb and Joshua. They will know who is with them like Elisha. They will keep their passion for God's cause like David.

The Cost of a Higher Perspective

It is costly to walk in divine perspective. You won't fit in the crowd anymore. You will have to deny your fears and learn how to encourage yourself in the Lord. You must continue to pursue the presence of the LORD to keep your passion pure.

A few years ago, I was facing a tremendous challenge. The ministry was prospering and the demands were growing greater every day. I found myself becoming weary of the number of people who needed me and the greater preaching load I faced. Looking for available time I allowed my devotional life to suffer. I took the time for people, sermon preparations and administrative duties. Unfortunately, this diligent seeker became too tired to seek. I was sinking to earthbound perspectives. There wasn't enough time, money or resources to accomplish the will of God.

At my worst moment, I had to fulfill my responsibilities as a minister in a conference. As I sat on the platform during one of the sessions feeling weak and discouraged, the minister spoke a word that changed my life. In the context of the parable of the wise and foolish virgins, she encouraged us to keep our lamps full of oil. And then, she made this statement, "Never get tired of buying the oil."

At that moment, I realized I had grown weary of paying the price for the greater demand. It seems when we are new in the things of God, the oil is relatively inexpensive. But, as we go on to know the Lord, our obedience becomes more expensive. To whom much is given, much is required.

Kathryn Kuhlman was asked once to comment on the price she had to pay for the anointing upon her life. Her response was, "It has cost me everything." The truth was that she was in love with a man who was not God's will for her life. Her obedience cost her the man she loved. However, her obedience purchased and released a flow of healing that touched millions. In the end, whatever you have to pay for the oil is well worth the price.

When you turn to see the voice, you embark upon a journey of great sacrifice and greater reward. David wanted to make an offering to the Lord. Ornan owned a threshing floor that could be used for the altar and oxen that could be used for the sacrifice. When he was approached by the king to buy his threshing floor, Ornan tried to give David everything he would need for his altar and offering.

> *Then David said to Ornan, "Give me the site of {this} threshing floor, that I may build on it an altar to the LORD; for the full price you shall give it to me, that the plague may be restrained from the people."*

And Ornan said to David, "Take {it} for yourself; and let my lord the king do what is good in his sight. See, I will give the oxen for burnt offerings and the threshing sledges for wood and the wheat for the grain offering; I will give {it} all."

> *But King David said to Ornan, "No, but I will surely buy {it} for the full price; for I will not take what is yours for the LORD, or offer a burnt offering which costs me nothing.* (1 *Chronicles* 21:22-24)

The face of God will not be revealed for those who are looking for a discount. The full price is required. But, for those who have tasted of His goodness and have caught a glimpse of His face, there is no other way.

Ask yourself:

- Are you desperately seeking the presence of God?
- Are you willing to leave the comfort of the old perspectives for the risks of a higher perspective—God's perspective.
- Will you pay the price for seeing His voice?

The desperate seeker will not be satisfied with a casual encounter. Those who passionately seek His face must place a demand upon His presence. And, for those who will turn to see His voice, He is your reward.